John H. Sheffield

Substance of the Speech of the Right Honourable Lord Sheffield

Monday, April 22, 1799, upon the subject of union with Ireland

John H. Sheffield

Substance of the Speech of the Right Honourable Lord Sheffield
Monday, April 22, 1799, upon the subject of union with Ireland

ISBN/EAN: 9783337195502

Printed in Europe, USA, Canada, Australia, Japan

Cover: Foto ©Andreas Hilbeck / pixelio.de

More available books at **www.hansebooks.com**

SUBSTANCE

OF THE

SPEECH

OF THE

RIGHT HONOURABLE

LORD SHEFFIELD,

Monday, April 22, 1799,

UPON THE SUBJECT OF

UNION WITH IRELAND.

LONDON:

Printed for J. DEBRETT, oppofite Burlington Houfe,
Piccadilly.

SUBSTANCE

OF THE

SPEECH

OF

LORD SHEFFIELD,

April 22, 1799.

&c. &c.

―――――――――

THE Chancellor of the Exchequer moved the order of the day for taking into confideration the Addrefs from the Lords upon the fubject of the Union with Ireland ; which being read, he moved that the faid Addrefs be now taken into confideration.

B

The Addreſs was then read twice, and the Chancellor of the Exchequer moved, That this Houſe do concur with the ſaid Addreſs.

Lord SHEFFIELD ſpoke as follows:

Mr. Speaker,

Sir, I wiſh it to be underſtood, that I ſupport the reſolutions and addreſs, in confidence that the aſſurance given by a noble Lord in an official ſituation in Ireland will be ſtrictly obſerved, namely, that Miniſters will *look to the ſenſe of Parliament and of the Country*, before the meaſure of Union ſhall again be brought forward there; and that aſſurance being given, I am not ſenſible of any ſufficient argument that ſhould prevent the Britiſh Parliament from giving ſome general explanation of the arrangement it is diſpoſed to make, more eſpecially as I obferve that fcarcely any man in this country objects to the principle of the meafure; nor can I fuppofe, that a nation fo well informed and fo much accuftomed to political confiderations as the Irifh, fhould for a long time perfevere in refufing to receive or examine what may be propofed from the Britifh Parliament; and for thefe reafons I wifh to trouble the Houfe with a few obfervations.

We cannot be much furprized at the alarm which has taken place in Ireland. The word Union was fuffered to be banded about there for many months without the flighteft attempt on the part of the Minifters to explain the terms of it. The aid of defigning men, and of thofe prejudiced from partial and local confiderations, was fcarcely neceffary to take advantage of this circumftance: the apprehenfions of Ireland

had always been, that an equal and favourable Union would not be granted : and no
fmall part of that people were made to believe, that their liberty, their independence,
their dignity, and almoſt the exiſtence of
the nation, would be done away by their
becoming one and the fame with the moſt
independent and moſt refpectable nation in
the world.

But, in truth, the meafure of Union was
ill-prepared for Ireland, and Ireland was ill-
prepared for Union. It is not without com-
petent information that I am convinced, if
the outline of the liberal propoſition for
Union, which is now offered, had been at
firſt properly communicated and with all
the plainnefs and candour which fuit the
Iriſh character, it would have been very
differently received ; and it is not my opinion alone, but the opinion alfo of thofe

who are not friendly to the meafure, that it might have been accepted, at leaft it would have prevented all that mifreprefentation and mifapprehenfion which might well be expected, without fome previous attention. I can hardly imagine a cafe, in refpect to which, until underftood, more jealoufy was likely to be entertained than this of a legiflative Union, otherwife the meafure being really fo neceffary and fo advantageous to Ireland, the ftrange abufe of the words " Dignity and Independence," which have been fo entirely miftaken there would have made little impreffion. I can fuppofe it will be unpleafing at firft to acknowledge, that the premature oppofition was the refult of an ill-founded jealoufy. Yet that acknowledgment, and the confequent departure from an *hafty* oppofition to the meafure, is no more than may be fairly expected from the candid opennefs of the Irifh character.

It is not now the queftion whether the meafure has been brought forward and con-ducted as it fhould have been, but whether the Britifh Parliament fhould do what de-pends on it to obviate the mifchief which muft arife from independent and feparate Legiflatures exifting within the fame empire, whether we fhould relinquifh a meafure which feems neceffary to the general fecu-rity and welfare, or take the prefent op-portunity of ftating the outline of it.

I fhall not trouble the Houfe with a re-petition of hiftorical inquiry into the caufes of the prefent ftate of Ireland, nor with many references to the reports of the Lords and Commons of that kingdom. The caufes and the proofs are but too plain. The noto-riety of numberlefs melancholy facts, which demonftrate the wretched and dangerous condition of that country, with reafon alarms every thinking man : it is an unanimous opinion in this country, that fomething is neceffary to be done to preferve Ireland ; and there feems to be almoft a general con- viction, that it can be done only by a legif- lative Union.

For my part, I cannot fee the meafure in any other light than that of being abfo- lutely neceffary. It has long been my opinion, and every thing which has hap- pened *in* Ireland, and in refpect to Ireland during the laft twenty years, particularly that which took place in 1782, and was whimfically enough called " Final Adjuft- ment," have convinced me of that neceffity.

When it was found proper to take off the fhackles from the Irifh Parliament, and highly proper it was, a Union fhould have been propofed, and by the fame meafure

only fhould all the commercial and other
advantages have been communicated, which
were fo indifcriminately conceded without
terms fince 1778. It would have been
ftill better, if an Union had taken place in
the beginning of the century, and that the
Conftitution and Commerce of Great Britain, which had been fo long and fo invi-
dioufly withheld, had been then communicated to Ireland. But in 1782, the admi-
niftration of that day, without fupplying
any means of keeping thefe kingdoms
together, rafhly gave away the depend-
ance of the two iflands on each other; and
now there is no certainty in the connexion
of Great Britain and Ireland. Independ-
ance of Legiflature feems to have fuggefted
notions of feparation, which appeared, in
fome degree, as early as 1784. However,
even thofe who attempt to juftify what was
done in 1782, muft acknowledge, that

there were points of effential confequence left unfettled, and that it fhould not have been poftponed to the hour of difficulty and diftrefs to arrange and afcertain the relative exertions and political connexions of the two countries.

Much has been faid on the words " Final Adjuftment : " but that which is fo called, only referred to the then afferted independence of Parliament, and by no means precluded Union : on the contrary, it was the opinion at the time, that *farther* meafures were neceffary to eftablifh a connexion on a folid and permanent bafis : and fo far as I underftand what was intended, I confider *that* adjuftment as putting the Irifh Parliament on the footing of independence and free deliberation, and in that fituation alone which could fatisfy the people of Ireland, that the acts of their Parliament would be thenceforward free and uncontrouled; but at any rate it is trifling to fuppofe, that nothing more was to be attempted, if that which had been done had not the effect of preferving the connexion and attachment of the two countries. It is true that Union became more neceffary, as well as more difficult, in confequence of what was done in 1782, and alfo in 1793, when the principle of our navigation and colonial laws were, without terms or occafion, facrificed by the act which permits goods and commodities of the growth, production, or manufacture, of Afia, Africa, or America, to be imported from Ireland into Great Britain. All thefe benefits fhould have been referved as the means of Union, but being then unconditionally granted, they have rendered that meafure much lefs fought for by Ireland; and I confefs that the ftrongeft objection I felt to the propofitions that were brought forward in the Britifh Parliament in 1785, (which by no means would have done what it is neceffary to do,) arofe from the apprehenfion, that if carried, they might prevent an Union. It was obvious, that if all the referved advantages of Great Britain were to be given up, there would be no means of future negotiation remaining.

Previoufly to that period, Ireland would have petitioned for an Union, and I think fhe might well do fo now as the greateft poffible acquifition fhe could make ; but neither the adjuftment in queftion, nor all the commercial conceffions, nor other means employed to tranquilize that country, have had the leaft effect. The bad ftate of Ireland yearly became worfe. It appears the parties are not to be fatisfied ; that no melioration of the condition of Ireland has taken place; that a great proportion of the people is now as ill difposed to Government, as bigoted, as ignorant, and as uncivilized as they were at the time of the maffacre in 1641. At prefent the permanency of the connexion of Great Britain with Ireland depends on the parties which exift, and ever muft exift, in a nation of Proteftants and Roman Catholics fo peculiarly interefted againft, and politically hoftile to, each other. Thefe divifions are the bane of the country, never to be annihilated but by a legiflative Union. The whole prefent fyftem is bad. The change of Government, at leaft every four years, and the conceffions fo regularly made under the vain notion of fatisfying the people, create and promote fchemes and fuggeftions inconfiftent with the tranquillity of the country, and encourage agitators, whofe uniform object it is, to disturb the public mind.

I have observed, that independence of Parliament suggested the idea of separation. Irrational notions of independence, leading to dissolution of Government, must end in civil war and the introduction of the French. Manufactures and agriculture would then cease much more suddenly than they could possibly revive; and whatever might be the event, Ireland would be completely ruined, and England greatly distressed. But supposing the crisis in question should not immediately come on, Ireland would continue in its present disturbed state, and England would ever find Ireland the back door to conspiracy, rebellion, and invasion. And so miserably distracted is Ireland at present, that among three millions of Roman Catholics, and half a million of Diffenters, there is fcarcely a man capable of a political idea, who does not wifh for fomething different from that which is; namely, a Change of the Church Eftablifhment, the Abolition of Tithes, a Parliamentary Reform, or a Republic : nor are the members of the eftablifhed Church entirely free from the fame un-happy temper of mind. The common Enemies of mankind will not fail to take advantage of this ftate of things : they have raifed it into a dangerous and formidable confpiracy, and it feems the only means through which they can hope of fucceed-ing in their favourite plan of deftroying the Britifh empire.

Nothing can be more dangerous than a notion, that a coalition of Churchmen, Diffenters, and Catholics, for the pur-pofe of feparation, cannot take place.

The reports of the Lords and Commons of Ireland, and what has happened lately, completely prove, that such a coalition is not merely possible, but that it actually exists, and that the foundations of it are laid, and deeply laid, already.

This subject has been so fully and so ably discussed, that it is not necessary to state how general, how great, and how irremediable by common means, are the mischief and danger : the unexampled perilous state of Ireland is well known : it was therefore evidently the duty of His Majesty's Ministers to bring forward some measure to prevent even the possibility of so great a calamity as the separation of the two countries ; and however I may differ in opinion with His Majesty's Ministers in respect to the conduct of this business, I acknowledge great merit in

their undertaking fuch an arduous tafk
at a time they were fo fully engaged in the
moft momentous concerns, and in their not
fhrinking from the difficulties which obvioufly might prefent themfelves, and which
too often induce Minifters to adopt fome
temporary expedient (juft to ferve their
turn) which never effectually fucceeds, but
in the end produces greater difficulty and
much mifchief. It feems alfo highly in-
cumbent on the Britifh Parliament to
take early the moft effectual fteps to promote the proper remedy : and every thing
has been tried, except that which is now
obvioufly the beft and only means, an
Union, and which, in confequence of the
wild opinions that are abroad, and the difturbed ftate of the world, has become ftill
more neceffary. Every conceffion has
been made, many colonial and commercial
advantages, which Ireland could not on

any reafonable ground claim without an Union, have been communicated to her: in fhort, every thing has been granted fo far, that we are now told by the enemies of Union, Ireland cannot acquire more by that meafure, and that fhe does not defire greater freedom and extenfion of trade, than fhe at prefent poffeffes, preferring her independence and dignity as a nation. They furely have odd notions of independence and dignity who prefer holding almoft the whole of their trade, almoft their exiftence at the difcretion of another country, rather than by *right* as a part of that country.

But I fhould not do juftice if I did not acknowledge this way of thinking is by no means general, and that the two largeft counties, Cork and Galway, and the city of Cork, county of Clare, and other diftricts of Ireland, had expreffed the contrary, and fo well, that I wifh to make ufe of their own words. Speaking of Union, the county of Cork fays :

County of Cork. { We are firmly perfuaded it would add to the welfare, the credit, and the immediate profperity of Ireland, and that by the uniting our ftrength in the clofeft manner with the moft free, and moft happy people on earth, we fhould exert the beft poffible means in our power for preferving the fafety, the honour, and the fecurity of our deareft rights. Determined, therefore, as we are to ftand or fall with Great Britain, we look forward with the greateft anxiety to this connexion, as the moft effectual means of putting an end to all our factions and religious animofities, and of reconciling the people of Ireland to each other, by doing away all ill-founded jealoufies between fellow-fubjects.

We confider it as moft obvioufly and indifpenfably neceffary to the profperity of this kingdom in general, and to the reftoration of that tranquillity and induftry, which alone can render the inhabitant profperous and happy, and moft likely in its confequences to reclaim the deluded people from thofe habits of violence and outrage to a fenfe of their duty to the laws of their country, and the beft of Kings.

City of Cork. { To become a conftituent part of that empire, to whofe protection we owe our political exiftence, and whofe Conftitution is the admiration of the civilized world : to participate in thofe refources, which are inexhauftible : to become joint

proprietors of that navy, which is irrefiftible, and to
fhare in that commerce which knows no bounds, are
objects beyond which our moft fanguine wifhes for the
profperity of Ireland cannot poffibly extend : while the
profpect, which they hold forth of terminating the
jarring intcrefts of party, and reconciling the jealous dif-
tinctions of religion, promifes, a reftoration of that
tranquillity to which this country has been too long a
ftranger.

County of Galway. { We are perfuaded, that a legiflative Union with Great Bri-
tain, eftablifhed on terms of perfect equality, would in-
vigorate the refources, increafe the wealth, and add ma-
terially to the fecurity of both countries, enabling them
to oppofe their common enemy with increafed ftrength
and power, and moft effectually to defeat their object of
dividing the empire for the purpofe of fubduing it. To
confider this meafure as it effects either country fepa-
rately, we conceive to be a narrow view of its object :
but even in that confined fenfe of it, we are firmly convinced it would add to the welfare, the credit, and the
immediate profperity of Ireland : and we are of opinion,
that uniting our ftrength in the clofeft manner with the
wifeft, the freeft, and the happieft people upon earth,
with whom we muft neceffarily ftand or fall, is fo far
from a facrifice of the honour and independence of
Ireland, that it is the beft means left to us for preferving both.

Thefe addreffes are moft refpectably
figned ; and a third addrefs from the

county of Cork, nearly in the fame words, has the fignature of 373 of the principal Nobility, Bifhops, Magiftrates, Clergy, and perfons of property, both Proteftants and Catholics : and there is reafon to believe, that the fentiments therein expreffed are much more general in the feveral counties which have not addreffed than has been fuppofed.

Although Ireland has acquired much which fhould only have been conceded by Union, it is not true that fhe cannot obtain farther commercial advantages by that mea-fure. The beft market, that of Great Bri-tain, for all Irifh manufactures, is ftill re-ferved, except linens, and her linens are become one of the greateft manufactures in the world, entirely in confequence of having that market, and could never have been carried on to its prefent great extent, unless aided by the prompt payment of Great Britain, which in a great degree acts as a supply of capital *.

Six parts in seven of the whole exports of linen from Ireland are imported into Great Britain, and of the seventh part the

* The bounties on the export of Irish linens from hence at the same time that they give to Great Britain about an eight of the trade in those articles, encourage the manufacture in Ireland. The average of bounties on the export of linens for the last four years is nearly 34,700l. Irish linens exported from Great Britain

	Yards
on an average of the last four years, entitled to bounty - - - - - -	4,866,015
Ditto not entitled to bounty - - - -	964,507
Total of Irish linens exported from Great Britain - - - - - - - -	5,830,522

The duties laid on the import of foreign linens for the purpose of protecting the British linen manufacture are about 25 per cent. of their real value, and give almost the monopoly of the British market to many articles of the Irish linen manufacture. The duties paid on foreign linen used in this country, on the same average, amount to 115,000. If the same rate of duties had been laid on Irish linens imported and used in this island under the usual policy of protecting the British manufacture, as is done in all like cases, it would raise a revenue of about 650,000l.

greateſt proportion goes to America, including the Weſt Indies. On an average of
four years, ending the 25th of March 1798,

	Yards
were exported from Ireland	39,885,776
of which to Great Britain -	33,695,659
To the Britiſh Colonies in America and Iſlands in the Weſt Indies * - - - - -	1,285,998
To the States of America - -	4,012,519
To foreign parts of Europe and to Africa - - - - - -	891,530,

being about a 44th part of the whole
export of linens from Ireland.

Linens are the only Iriſh manufacture,
properly ſo called, which has the advantage of the Britiſh market, and it has flou-
riſhed accordingly. No manufacture, no
trade of Ireland, except ſuch as are duty

* In this are not included Iriſh linens exported from
Great Britain to the Britiſh Colonies and to the Ame-
rican States, but only the quantities ſent directly from
Ireland to the places mentioned.

free, or have particular advantages in the British market, have succeeded. Linens, corn, and the produce of cattle, which alone have those advantages, amount on an average of the last three years to 5,410,825 when the total value of all Irish imports into Great Britain were 5,612,689 of which there were articles not the manufacture and produce of Ireland to the amount of - - - - - - - - - - - - 101,864

So that the articles of Irish growth or manufacture, which are not duty free, or have no particular exemption or advantage in British ports, amount only to - - - - 100,781 and form a small proportion, indeed, of the great importation from Ireland into Great Britain alone amounting to 5,612,689, which, stated in the manner most favourable to Ireland, is, at least, six parts in seven of the whole export trade of Ireland to all parts.

We cannot be furprized, that woollen and other manufactures have decreafed in Ireland during the late turbulent ftate of that country. We may rather wonder, that they have not been more affected: but fuch articles as have the peculiar advantage of the Britifh market, have even lately increafed. The manufactures and commerce of Ireland are now, and have always been, greatly inferior to what they may be; it is reafonable therefore to fuppofe, that when the prefent prohibitory duties which were laid on manufactures coming from all parts to protect thofe of England, are, in refpect to Irifh manufactures, equalized, as intended by the articles of Union, and they fhall have the advantage of the Britifh market the fame as linens; the produce of cattle and corn, they may alfo flourifh.

No country is better circumftanced for manufactures than Ireland. She has plenty of water and fuel *, the firft requifites in

---

* Moft parts of Ireland, where, through want of fkill and wealth, they have not yet been able to fupply themfelves with coal, particularly the manufacturing dif- tricts, are acceffible by water and near the coafts of England and Wales, which abound in coals. Ireland may have that article cheaper from the Weft and North-weft of England and from Wales, than it can go coaftwife to many places in Great Britain where great manufactories are carried on which confume large quantities of that ar- ticle. Coals from Great Britain to Ireland pay only an export duty of 14d. per chaldron, when the fame article carried coaftwife to London pays a duty of 9s. 3d. per chaldron, and to any other part of England 5s. 9d. If Ireland does not think it neceffary to protect her own col- lieries by any import duty, fhe may cheapen the price of coals to her manufacturers by taking off the duty of 1s. 9½d. per ton on the import of that article into Dublin, and of 9½d. into all other parts of Ireland. The paffage from the Englifh collieries is fhort, and the freight is moderate. And it may be obferved, that inferior forts of coal anfwer the purpofe of manufacture, and that the bogs of Ireland furnifh plenty of excellent peat or turf.

manufactures. The encouragement to her
induſtry will be great, eſpecially as it will
be impoſſible to countervail the difference
of price of labour and of exciſes in the
two countries *, and commercial men will
acknowledge the ſuperior advantage of a
near market, and a quick return, ſo ab-
ſolutely neceſſary to a country wanting
capital.

If Union ſhould take place, there will be
no jealouſy, no warfare of bounties and
drawbacks, no invidious wiſh to check the
proſperity of Ireland, or any manufacture
there, and the great commercial advantages
of Ireland will no longer be held at the
pleaſure of another country.

---

* Import duties in the two countries may be equalized, or the difference of thoſe duties on raw materials
may be paid on import of the article or manufacture, of
which it is made.

The profperity of Ireland, fuch as it is, in no degree arofe from the independency of the Irifh Parliament, but from commercial advantages derived from Great Britain. I hefitated when I firft heard that a contrary affertion came from a man as able, as refpectable, and, at leaft, as well informed, as any in the two iflands; but the affertion that the profperity of Ireland arofe from the independence of her Parliament, appears to me fo entirely unfupported by fact, that I fcarcely know how to reafon about it, except by afking, whether the increafe of the linen manufacture; whether the profperity of the beef, pork, and butter-trade; whether the growth of a grain of corn, or of a blade of grafs; whether the opening of the ports of Great Britain to Irifh corn at a lower price than from other countries, have been effected by the independence of the Irifh Parliament: in fhort, which article

of growth or export has increafed in confequence of it ? Have the laws been better
executed ? Has the country been more
tranquil ? Are life and property more
fafe ? In truth, I can trace little to that
event but the prefent difturbed ftate of Ireland. I repeat, that the profperity of Ireland entirely depends on the connexion
with and advantages derived from Great
Britain, without which her trade would be
almoft nothing; and this appears fo perfectly evident, that I confider it not to
be neceffary to add a fyllable more to
prove it.

When Ireland has acquired the Britifh
Conftitution a due execution of laws and
tranquillity, and that life and property are fecure there, Englifh capitals will undoubtedly
be employed in Ireland, and then her profperity will be real and permanent. At pre-

fent no prudent man will lend one fhilling
to that country in any fhape, far lefs will a
commercial or manufacturing man rifk his
capital in any fpeculation, where a fpirit of
unfriendly independence, of feparation and
of rebellion fo ftrongly prevails; but furely
it is not commercial advantage and wealth
only that are wanting to Ireland. She is
deficient in the moft effential of all things,
good order and well-executed laws. Life
and property are not more fecure there, than
among the moft difturbed people upon
earth. A refidence there is as much to be
avoided as in countries fubject to the moft
hideous tyranny or favage banditti.

It is curious, efpecially at this time, that
apprehenfions are expreffed that the number of abfentees will be greatly increafed
by an Union. There are now infinitely a
greater number of Irifh emigrants, for the

fake of perfonal fafety, than will be occa-
fioned if Union fhould be adopted. If that
meafure fhould take place, few families will
follow thofe who are called to Parliament :
if they make the experiment, the difference
of expence will foon check the evil : and
thofe that occafionally become abfentees,
will be fo by choice, not by compulfion.

It will not be improper in this place to
ftate, with the view of removing wrong
impreffions, that the number and property
of abfentees have been always greatly ex-
aggerated, and alfo the bad effects of the
confequent drain of money.

Thofe who are moft capable of examining the queftion agree, that the remittance
to regular abfentees is below 600,000l., I
believe confiderably, which is not more
than one fifth of the value of the exports of

linens alone to this country, amounting to,
at leaft, three millions. According to the
common valuation, it may not always appear fo much, becaufe they are rated, at
moft, at 1s. 6d. per yard, even now that
their quality is much improved; but if
valued at only 19d., linen and linen yarn
will, on an average of the laft three years,
amount to a larger fum than I have mentioned, and more than balance all the imports of Great Britain; including raw materials, as well as remittances to abfentees.
The imports of the products and manufacture of Ireland into Great Britain on an
average of the laft three years,

being - - - - - - - - 5,510,825

and all imports of the produce
or manufacture of Great Britain into Ireland - - - - 2,087,672
                                      ——————
                                      3,425,153

So that there is a balance of upwards of
2,800,000 in favour of Ireland, allowing
an actual remittance of 600,000 l. to abfentees.

The above is the ſtatement of the interchange of produce and manufacture. . Be-
fides which, Ireland imports from Great
Britain at preſent, in confequence of her
being obliged to avail herſelf of Britiſh capital, and of her limited commerce, except
with Great Britain,

Of colonial articles - - - 970,000
Of foreign merchandize - - 498,173
_____
1,468,173

And England receives from
Ireland of colonial and foreign merchandize - - - 101,874
_____

which gives a balance to England on foreign and colonial
importation of - - - - 1,366,309
and if deducted from the above balance of

2,800,000, will still on the whole, stating the trade and remittances in the most favourable manner for Ireland, leave a balance of 1,433,691l. in favour of the latter country.

It should be observed, that while the imports of the produce and manufacture of Ireland into Great Britain are in a progressive state of certain increase, on the other hand, the imports of foreign and colonial articles from Great Britain into Ireland are in a course of decrease; but I proceed to considerations of more consequence to both countries.

I am little disposed to argue in favour of non-residence, but I must observe, that those parts of Ireland, as well as of England, where manufactures flourish, are remarkable for the non-residence of land-proprietors. Yet, in other parts of the

F

country, I confider their abfence as the greateft misfortune, and I conceive one of the moft effential advantages of England over Ireland arifes from the refidence of that clafs of men, and from their great attention to the people, and to all the details of the country round them. But we cannot be furprized, that men of fortune in Ireland fhould now refide in villas near the metropolis, or abfent themfelves, when we recollect the uncivilized ftate of the country. At prefent it cannot be expected from them, nor is it fafe, and unlefs fome great change fhould happen, which will induce and enable men of fortune to live there, and to inftruct, protect, and encourage the people, civilization will go on very flowly.

All the fame objections which are urged in Ireland againft an Union, were made by

Scotland at the time of her Union with
England, and every mifchief was pre-
dicted, but they all proved unfounded.
Arguments, which came from fome of the
ableft men of thofe times, and which then
appeared almoft conclufive, are completely
refuted by experience. It was faid, that
Edinburgh would be deferted and ruined :
the fame is now faid of Dublin : but fince
Union, the fize of Edinburgh, and the
number of her inhabitants, have been more
than doubled, and the city beautified in a
high degree. All Scotland is greatly
improved, her population increafed, fhe is
ten times more rich fince that period : her
people are civilized, the laws are now executed, life and property are fecure; the Legiflatures of the two Kingdoms no longer
at variance as heretofore, and at the rifk of
rupture each counteracting the other. Few
families of property are now conftantly

abfentees, and almoft without exception, thofe Scotchmen, who go from home and acquire a fortune, in the end carry it to Scotland. Before the Union, Scotland had fcarcely any thing worthy the name of a manufacture: all her efforts to obtain a foreign or colonial trade had failed, but now her manufactures and trade are as great in proportion as thofe of England. And all thefe advantages are greatly beyond the progreffive improvement which would have taken place without an Union, and without which many of them never could have taken place.

The alarm in the city of Dublin on the fubject of Union is faid to be greater and more juft than elfewhere, but I am perfectly fatisfied that her apprehenfions are unfounded. The abfence of 80 Commoners and 30 Lords, even fuppofing them conftantly resident before, certainly cannot ruin Dublin. The Lord Lieutenant, the principal officers of every kind, the Courts of Justice will still remain. She will still continue the Winter residence of the principal people of fortune, as Edinburgh does. She will be the seat of education, of amusement, and of the arts. Her trade will increase greatly. The complete intercourse and exchange of commodities which will be established by an Union, will raise her commerce beyond what the most sanguine man has ever yet imagined. Cork, Waterford, and Limerick, will have a great proportion of the provision and other trade; but Dublin will be the great mart for the import and export, particularly of manufactures. Dublin will have the great trade to the most thriving port, perhaps, in the world; I mean Liverpool. The trade of Ireland with England will be carried on with most security, especially in time of war, between thofe ports. Every article of foreign and Britifh manufacture and produce which Ireland does not furnifh or import immediately from the place of growth or of manufacture, fhe may have from thence. Almoft all the widely-extended inland navigation of England points to Liverpool, and may fupply what is wanted to advantage. As Ireland imports but a fmall proportion of her confumption of Weft-India articles directly from the place of growth, Dublin is well fituated for fupplies of thofe articles from Briftol and Liverpool in return for her exports to thofe places. The corn trade will become a prodigious article, if the produce of the two iflands fhould by an Union be put on the fame footing as between two counties in England. The great inland navigations of Ireland will convey corn at a cheaper rate to Dublin, even from Limerick and Connaught, much cheaper than by a circuitous and precarious voyage by fea. The canal tolls on corn and flour fhould, in favour of Dublin, be purchafed at the public expence, or greatly reduced; and the fame fhould be done in refpect to the docks in the port of Dublin. This would facilitate the intercourfe between the two countries, and be a mutual advantage to them both; and would ultimately benefit Dublin much more than the refidence of thofe who would be fent to the united Parliament. Dublin would become the warehoufe of the corn of that kingdom for the fteady and certain corn markets of the North-weft of Great Britain and the North of Ireland, where a very fmall part of the confumption of the inhabitants can poffibly be grown. The Englifh farmer may at firft be alarmed, when he hears, that Ireland will be confidered as a part of

England in refpect to the corn-trade; but the advantages will be reciprocal, and the effect, which fome may apprehend from an influx of corn more than fufficient, cannot take place. Unfortunately we conftantly import as much oats as Ireland can fpare at any time, at prefent double the quantity, and that evil is increafing rather than decreafing. She is well fituated to furnifh that part of Great Britain, which will always require a fupply of that kind of corn, and the quantity of wheat fhe is ever likely to fpare will not be fufficient to overload the Britifh markets. It will be much lefs mifchievous to the growers of wheat in England to have the ports regularly and conftantly open to the limited quantity that can come from Ireland, than to have them open to a glut of corn from all parts of the world for three months certain; the moment the fmalleft proportion of the confumption of this country is wanting, the moment its price becomes what is by no means extravagant, but on the contrary, while it is moderate, confidering the increafed expence of tillage. The opening of our ports for three months certain to all the world, when we only want a moderate quantity, may reduce the price of wheat ruinoufly low; but the comparatively fmall quantity that could come from Ireland, would have no farther effect than fupplying what may be actually wanted. When Ireland has a conftantly open market in Great Britain for corn, it will prove the greateft encouragement to her farmers to change their flovenly management. At prefent their corn is exported in fo bad a ftate, that it muft meet the corn of other countries at market to great difadvantage. When they have a fteady market, they will foon find the ne-

ceffity of preparing and dreffing their corn
in a manner that will enable it to bear a
competition with the corn of England.

It has been fuggefted, that the manufactures of Ireland, and particularly the
linen trade, would fuffer through the want
of a refident Parliament. The principal
manufactures and commerce of Scotland
are fituated at a greater diftance from London than thofe of Ireland, and they became
what they are fince the Union of the Parliaments; yet there has never been the flighteft
complaint in refpect to neceffary protection
and affiftance from the Britifh Parliament:
and perhaps it may not improperly be obferved in this place, that no difadvantage
whatever has arifen to the affairs of Scotland
in confequence of her having only forty-
five Members in the Britifh Parliament,
but they have been as well attended to

and as well managed as thofe of England by upwards of five hundred Members, and the government of Scotland has been ad-miniftered fince Union as vigilantly and more impartially than before, and the fame, in all probability, will be the cafe in refpect to Ireland.

The objection to Union on the part of the Proteftants of Ireland is unaccountable : they can hardly be faid to conftitute a na-tion : they are an Englifh colony govern-ing upwards of three millions of Roman Catholics, or, at leaft, fix times their own number in a country acquired and main-tained by Englifh arms and treafure, which colony never could have fupported itfelf; and even the laft Summer would have been overwhelmed, unlefs protected by the fame means by Englifh power. They cannot difdain that defcription; many of them, I

am fure, are fenfible, that fuch is their
fituation, and that their confequence and
fecurity depend on the connexion with the
Mother Country. In refpect to the Roman
Catholics, Union alone can make it fafe to
fatisfy their claims. By Union, all that
enmity, jealoufy, and contrariety of in-
tereft, which naturally arife between thofe
two unequal bodies, muft foon ceafe. The
Proteftants will lofe nothing ; I am fatisfied their object was not monopoly, but
fafety : they will be fafe, and relieved from
all apprehenfions, and may have a better
tenantry, and more attached to their in-
tereft. The Roman Catholics may acquire
all they can defire; and I hope we fhall
never again hear of Proteftant afcendancy
or Catholic emancipation, words which
have been very infidioufly employed to the
worft purpofes. On cool reflexion it will
appear, that Ireland will not incur any

difadvantage, but the advantages to be gained by her are the greateft that can be conceived, and, in the firft place, fecurity and tranquillity, as it is reafonable to fuppofe, that an identity of Conftitution and a due execution of the Laws, will produce the fame effects in Ireland as they have done in Great Britain, and particularly in Scotland within this century. Till Union takes places, and not till then, will the theoretical independence of Ireland become practical. Ireland, in truth, is now actually dependent on England through her divifions, through her trade, and through her Conftitution. Either the Proteftants or the Catholics will depend on Englifh fupport. It has been fhewn, that the trade of Ireland is abfolutely dependent on that of England; and the King of Great Britain being fubject to Britifh laws, in obeying him, and under the

neceſſary controul of his Miniſters, Ireland
muſt in ſome ſort be dependent : but ſup-
poſing two perfectly independent Legiſla-
tures within the ſame empire, they muſt
always be conſidered as in an uncertain and
perilous ſtate, mutually inconvenient to
each other, and always cheriſhing diſcon-
tent and jealouſy. If one Parliament exerts
powers in oppoſition to thoſe of the other,
what muſt be the conſequences ? They
are ſo obvious, that it would be an abuſe of
time to ſtate them. We cannot reflect
with much ſatisfaction on the only two in-
ſtances which have occurred ſince the independence of the Iriſh Legiſlature, where-
in the two Parliaments could act oppoſitely
to each other. The rejection of the commercial propoſitions in 1785, on the part
of Ireland, has not obtained the applauſe,
even in that country, of the well-informed,
and the conduct which was held on the

occafion of appointing a Regency evinced a difpofition to rifk the mifchiefs which might be expected to arife from the clafhing of two independent Parliaments. In fhort, if the fort of independence which is claimed has any meaning, it leads to feparation— Union or feparation muft take place; for it feems agreed on all fides, that the countries cannot go on as they are.

Soon after the acceffion of James the Firft to the Thrones of thefe kingdoms, that wife Statefman and Counfellor, Sir Francis Bacon, ftrongly recommended an Union between England and Scotland. He clearly faw how faulty and precarious the fortunate junction of the two countries would be, if only fupported by the circumftance of having the fame King. He propofed a complete Union. He recommends highly the liberal fyftem of the

Romans, obferving, that their naturaliza-
tions were, in effect, perpetual mixtures,
not only with perfons, but with cities and
countries ; and adds, that there never were
any States that were good commixtures but
the Romans. He alfo obferves, that the
conduct of other kingdoms has been different, and confequently the addition of
farther empire and territory has been rather matter of burden than of ftrength, and
kept alive the feeds of revolt and rebellion
for many ages. And he adds, that Arragon
was united to Caftile by a marriage ; but
after an hundred years, a civil war com-
menced in confequence of the bad policy of
not incorporating, but leaving it a feparate
Government ; and if he had lived as late
as thefe times, he might have ftated
much ftronger cafes. Machiavel alfo at-
tributes the growth of the Roman Empire to the good policy in incorporating

fo eafily with ftrangers; and Molyneux, the ftrenuous afferter of the independence of the Irifh Parliament, fays, an Union on equal terms would be highly advantageous to Ireland, and the beft means of enjoying that independence : and the Irifh Parliament, in the beginning of this century, expreffed a defire for an entire Union. But the times were not fo enlightened as they now are, and a narrow policy prevented the participation of thofe liberal, fair, and equal terms, which are now offered to Ireland. The prefent Chief Baron of Ireland, one of the firft conftitutional authorities of that kingdom, and a fuccefsful fupporter of Irifh independence in 1782, has afferted, that the independence of the Irifh Parliament was moft valuable, becaufe it would enable Ireland to treat for a Union upon fair terms.

H

The Union of Wales and Scotland with
England, the Union of Bretagne, Dauphiny,
and other provinces with France, the
Union of the feveral kingdoms of Spain,
all of which, while independent, were
greatly prejudicial to each other, proved
highly advantageous to the different countries and to the empires, in proportion to
the completenefs of legiflative Union that
took place ; and the fenfible Americans
foon difcovered how dangerous their fituation would be, if they remained feparate
independent States.

Every advantage that was expected, and
more than was expected, has been derived
from the Union of Scotland. No country
was ever more difturbed before and at the
time. Nothing could tend more directly
to feparation than the act of fecurity which
paffed in the Parliament of Scotland juft

before that event : a great proportion of the
people of all ranks were as ill-difpofed to-
wards England as the worſt difpofed of the
Iriſh. The Clans were as much out of the
reach of the law as any part of Ireland can
be fuppofed to be. To carry fire and fword
from one diſtrict into another, was as much
the difpofition of the Highlanders, as it has
been lately of White-boys and Defenders in
Ireland. The taſte and faſhion of the people
were to be in a fituation to commit hofti-
lities, and the chief men of the country,
inftead of endeavouring to excite the induſtry of their dependants, only valued
themfelves in proportion to the number of
thofe who were difpofed to follow them in
arms. Notwithſtanding the Crowns of the
two kingdoms had been annexed above an
hundred years, a connexion with France
was ftill kept up, and the moft dangerous
intrigues carried on. I fhall only add, that

although the caufes or motives were not
precifely the fame, the effects were; and
many other inftances of the diforders,
and of the refemblance of the fituation
of Scotland at that time to the prefent
ftate of Ireland might eafily be ftated,
and that all thofe circumftances which
difturbed Scotland, as much as Ireland now
is, have been done away by Union.

Nature has given many local advantages to Ireland. Union will give her a
Conftitution that is deemed the beft; will
give her tranquillity, wealth, and character; and money will be lent in Ireland,
when fettled, with as much confidence as
in England. Thofe who are now abfentees
would find the advantage of refiding there.
Englifhmen would rifk their perfons and
property in that country, which, if not

immediately, will in time, become as civilized as Great Britain.

On the whole, it may be confidently pronounced, Union is moſt neceſſary, and will be moſt beneficial to Ireland. The plan ſeems formed for her peculiar, although I will not ſay for her excluſive, advantage, and as a partial friend I could not propoſe any thing more favourable for her. Yet it by no means follows, that the great advantages of Union to Ireland will be counterbalanced by diſadvantages to Great Britain, or that the gain of Ireland will be the loſs of Great Britain. In a long courſe of years, even if the meaſure of Union ſhould not take place, manufactures and trade will decline in ſome places when they redouble from various circumſtances in others : but poſſible local diſadvantages muſt not prevent the Legiſlature from looking to the general goo'. It muſt be admitted, the proſperity of I land would be the proſperity of Great P . tain. The inefficient ſtate ot a po n a great loſs to the whole. The different ed ſtate of that country is a general d ack from the proſperity of the empire every part of which will find the advantage of that high degree of improvement which the affimilation of the two countries would effect. Great additional ſtrength, and ſecurity and general proſperity to Great Britain and to the Empire, will be the conſequence of Union, and the attention of the Executive Government would not hereafter, amidſt the diſtreſſes of war, and at the moment of the utmoſt peril, be diſtracted by conſpiracies and rebellion in Ireland.

Perhaps no circumſtance in the character

of the commercial and manufacturing in-
terefts, and of the people in general in
Great Britain, gives a greater proof of
their liberality and good fenfe, than their
acquiefcence on this occafion in fome poffible facrifice of manufactures, of commerce, and of conftitution, for the fake
of unity and tranquillity of empire:
The energies of commerce furpafs, and
fometimes contradict, the moft plaufible
calculations : and even in a commercial
light England might be benefited by a
great increafe of manufactures and commerce in Ireland, inafmuch as Ireland will
be better enabled to pay for the many
articles fhe will continue to take from
England. We all know that much commercial advantage cannot be obtained by
trading with a nation which is not rich,
efpecially when the produce of the two
countries is the fame. The interchange of

commodities will animate trade; and no intelligent man will fay, that the manu- factures of England have decreafed in con- fequence of the great increafe of manufac- tures in Scotland. But thofe who will give themfelves the trouble of examining the queftion will find, that the two countries are mutually benefited by the profperous ftate of their refpective manufactures and commerce, and that competition encourages fkill and induftry, and promotes and en- forces good regulations, and confequent cheapnefs of manufacture. In refpect to revenue, the empire will be highly be- nefited; for with the increafe of wealth, there will be as great increafe in the ex- cife and cuftoms; and when we enu- merate the commercial and other ad- vantages that would be derived from an Union, we fhould not forget the mif- chiefs that would be avoided, and that the final termination of the antient alliances, 'the connexion, and the intrigues of France with Scotland, and all projects of separation, were at last effected by the Union of Great Britain.

In respect to the incompetence of Parliment, it is difficult to believe that that objection is at this time seriously urged : if it is, it only convinces me there is great want of argument against the measure of Union. The argument would throw us back to first principles ; that is, the dissolution of Government, and to that jargon which has nearly ruined Europe. This doctrine was ably refuted at the time of the Union with Scotland ; if it had not, it would ill suit the pretensions of Ireland to establish it.

If I should be asked, whether I am satis-

fied that Union will produce order and
fteady profperity in Ireland, I fhould anfwer, that I am. The fame violence and
machinations which exift at prefent to effect feparation might poffibly be attempted
at firft; but when Ireland is irrevocably
become a part of Great Britain, there would
gradually and foon be an end of fpeculations
and confpiracies. France would no longer
fpeculate on diftinct governments and in-
terefts. The enemies of order would not
be tempted by any profpect of fuccefs:
they would recollect, that it is not Ireland
alone, but the three kingdoms, that muft
be induced to facrifice or yield their Conftitution: and, as was the cafe in Scotland,
when the people of that country, who had
been fo averfe to Union, had tafted the
fweets of that meafure, they became the
moft ftrenuous fupporters of it ; info-
much, that when it was the object to raife

a rebellion there, it was found that a decla-
ration againſt Union would be unpopular
and hurt the cauſe.

It may appear extraordinary, that ſo
much ſhould be ſaid in this Houſe to prove
the advantage of Union to Ireland ; but
the arguments are not ſo miſapplied as they
may ſeem to be, they are, in truth, arguments
to recommend the laying a propoſition before the Iriſh nation ſo beneficial, that I cannot doubt but a people of great abilities
and capable of diſcernment, will, when the
heat of their alarm has ſubſided, no longer
refuſe to take into conſideration a plan
which may be highly advantageous to every
part of the empire ; and unleſs the meaſure
had been ill underſtood, the unreaſonable
refuſal to liſten to any propoſition, could
not have taken place.

In voting for the refolutions, I do not mean to approve more than the *principle* of Union, to which no adequate objection has been ftated. If we fhould hereafter proceed to details, it will be then neceffary to give all our attention, and exert our beft powers in examining the articles; and above all, in preventing harm to the Conftitution, taking care that we do not, with a levity and fubmiffion that feem to belong to the times, do any thing that may be unneceffary for one country, and fhould be highly dreaded by the other.

There has now been an opportunity of fome experience, which it is to be hoped will promote the utmoft liberality and candour in propofing the meafure, whenever the people of Ireland are found to be difpofed to accept it. Every man will agree with me in deprecating all idea of force or threats, or the ufe of any means that are not perfectly fair and honourable.

To render Union fatisfactory and permanent, it will not be fufficient that it be merely acceded to by Parliament. The people at large muft be reconciled to it; and that they may, is the wifh neareft my heart. It is for Ireland that I am moft interefted on this occafion. Her deplorable condition demands it; for I am moft ferioufly convinced the meafure is *abfolutely neceffary for her tranquillity, fecurity, and welfare.* The bad effects of two feparate Parliaments within one empire, and the baneful idea of feparation, can be done away only by an Union; and until that event takes place, Ireland will never be fettled, will always be difturbed by the moft mifchievous fpeculations and intrigues, the ſport of parties, and of the enemies of England; ſhe will be a weakneſs as ſhe is at preſent, inſtead of a ſtrength to the empire.

THE END.

www.ingramcontent.com/pod-product-compliance
Lightning Source LLC
Chambersburg PA
CBHW021630270326
41931CB00008B/948